Monkey Says

Written by Gill Budgell
Illustrated by Denise Hughes

sit

pat

get up

rub

nod

Talk about the book

Ask your child these questions:

1 What are the children doing at the beginning of the book?

2 What does Monkey pat?

3 Which part of the body do you use to nod?

4 Which action does Monkey not do?

5 Can you think of a game that is like Monkey Says?

6 Have you ever played a game like Monkey Says/Simon Says?